# Exploring Inner Space

## By M. C. Hall

**Scott Foresman**
is an imprint of

Glenview, Illinois • Boston, Massachusetts • Chandler, Arizona •
Upper Saddle River, New Jersey

**Photographs**

Every effort has been made to secure permission and provide appropriate credit for photographic material. The publisher deeply regrets any omission and pledges to correct errors called to its attention in subsequent editions.

Unless otherwise acknowledged, all photographs are the property of Pearson Education, Inc.

Photo locators denoted as follows: Top (T), Center (C), Bottom (B), Left (L), Right (R), Background (Bkgd)

**Opener:** National Park Service; **1** ©James Stevenson/©DK Images; **3** (Bkgd) ©Chris Howes/Wild Places Photography/Alamy Images, (Inset) ©NASA; **4** ©James Stevenson/©DK Images; **6** ©Roger Ressmeyer/Corbis; **7** ©DK Images; **8** ©Larry Lee Photography/Corbis; **9** (B) ©Michael Nichols/National Geographic Image Collection, (T) SuperStock; **10** ©Mark Cosslett/National Geographic Image Collection; **11** National Park Service; **12** ©Photo Resource Hawaii/Alamy Images.

ISBN 13: 978-0-328-47265-9
ISBN 10:  0-328-47265-4

**Pearson®** is a trademark, in the U.S. and/or in other countries, of Pearson plc or its affiliates.
**Scott Foresman®** is a trademark, in the U.S. and/or in other countries, of Pearson Education, Inc., or its affiliates.

2 3 4 5 6 7 8 9 10 V010 13 12 11 10

Some adventurers explore outer space. They blast off to visit the moon or the space station.

Other adventurers explore inner space. They go underground into caves and tunnels inside Earth.

outer space

inner space

# What is inside Earth?

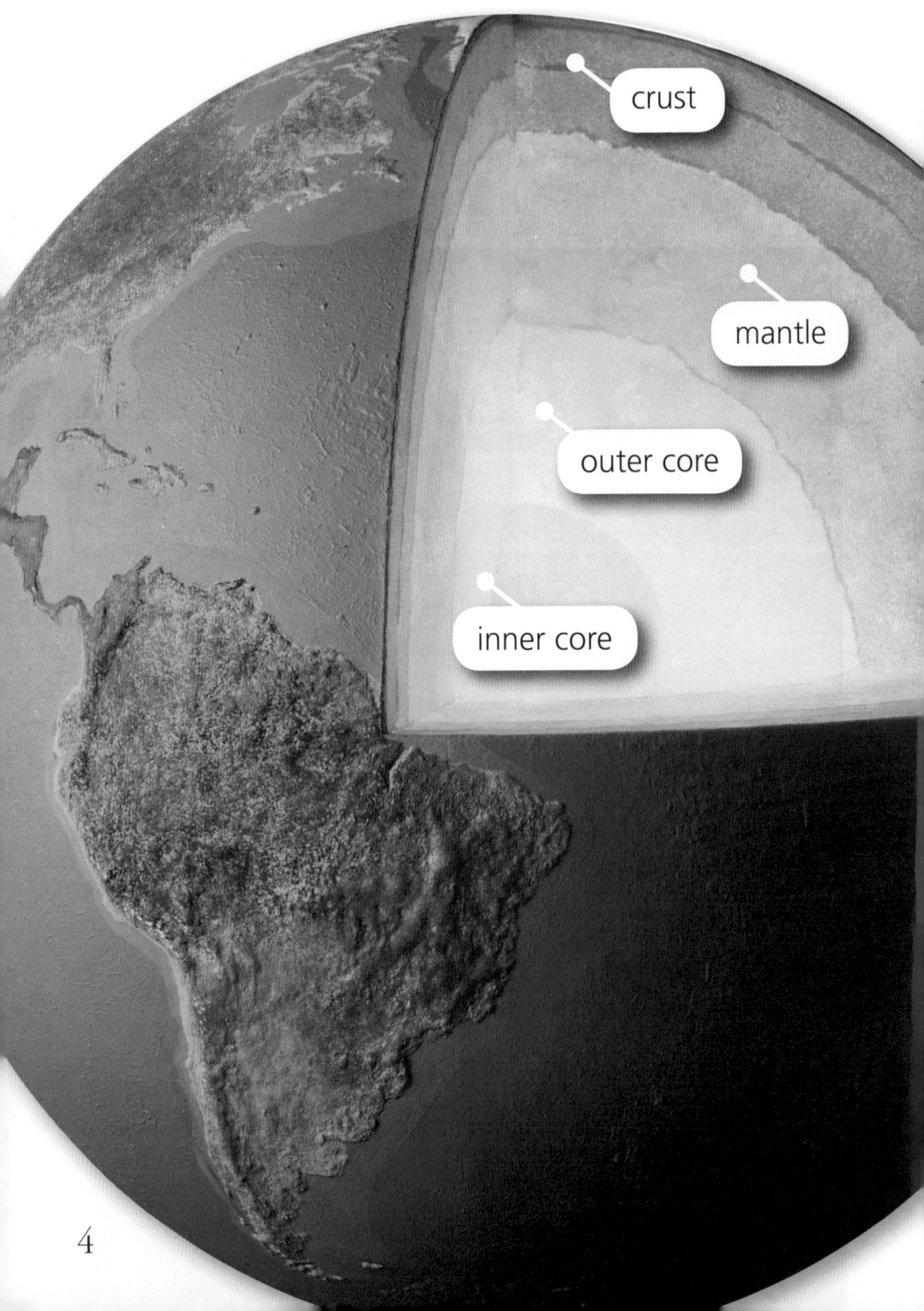

crust

mantle

outer core

inner core

Our planet is made of layers. The crust is Earth's outside layer. It's made of rocks and soil.

The mantle is the middle layer. It's much thicker than the crust. The rocks there are hot and soft. The melted rocks of the mantle are called *magma*. When magma rises to the surface, it erupts from a volcano. Then it is called *lava*.

The innermost layer, the core, is very dense and very hot.

Even the bravest explorers can't go deeper than the crust. But scientists have many questions about Earth's center.

Scientists study volcanoes to learn about inner Earth. When a volcano erupts, rocks, ash, and hot gasses from the mantle come out of it. Lava flows from some erupting volcanoes.

Scientists who study volcanoes are called volcanologists.

Scientists set up machines to measure earthquakes in different places.

Scientists also use computers to study inner space. The computers keep track of thousands of earthquakes all around the world. The computers use that information to make pictures of Earth's center.

Does anyone explore beneath Earth's surface? Miners dig tunnels deep into Earth's crust. They dig out minerals such as gold, coal, and iron.

Huge drills dig mining tunnels.

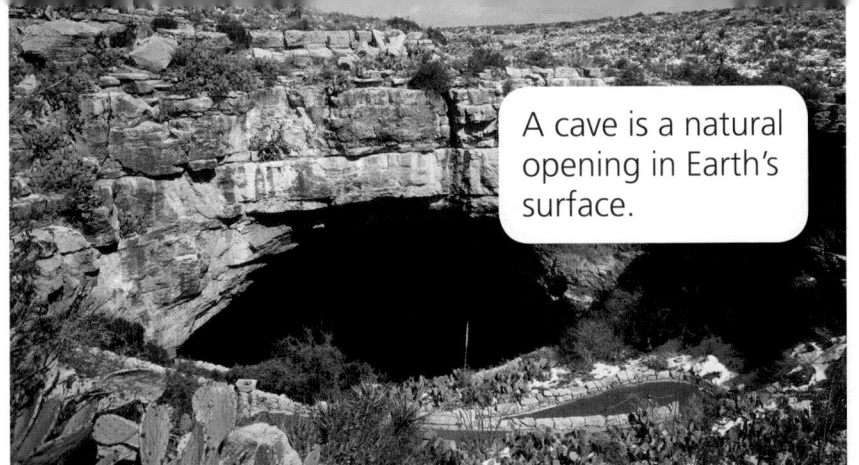

A cave is a natural opening in Earth's surface.

It took many years for this strange sight to form!

Adventurers go deep into underground caves to see what it's like there.

It's dark underground. Miners and cave explorers have to bring lights with them. If they lose their way, they may never get out!

Cave explorers can get into tight spots!

At Carlsbad Caverns National Park, rangers lead visitors through parts of the cave.

Would you like to explore inside Earth's crust? Some caves and mines are open to visitors. Marked trails, boardwalks, and lights make these places safer than they used to be.

And if you're in Hawaii, you can visit a real volcano! Just don't get too close!

Lava flow from Mount Kilauea in Hawai'i Volcanoes National Park